Leave on E: Poems of
Power, *Passion*, Purpose,
and
Perspective

Gnatee Doe

While the author has made every effort to provide accurate contact information at the time of publication, neither the publisher nor the author assumes any responsibility for errors, or for changes that occur after publication. Further, the publisher does not have any control over and does not assume any responsibility for author or third-party websites or their content.

The author uses words or language that are considered profane, vulgar, or offensive by some readers.

Printed in the United States of America

First Printing, 2018

ISBN-13: 978-0998988917
ISBN-10: 099898891X
Library of Congress Control Number: 2017918773

Convexed Cognitive Publications
1479 Shady Pl #4108
Daytona Beach, FL 32114
convexedcognition@gmail.com

A copy of this book may be purchased on Amazon.com

Author Photograph by Selina Puentes

Introduction

Initially thought of as my second (stand-alone) book of poetry, this volume is the beginning of a series that will span the rest of my life.

When I think of **power**, I think of it as a derivative from the ability to invoke. More than just "will power", because power is a manifestation of will. My will drives my focus, to speak and create things into existence.

Passion, if not tamed, may be unbridled and unpredictable. However, when it is placed in the right position, what it yields is promising and life changing.

When I know why I was designed, my destination is unveiled. Discovering my **purpose**, allows me to acknowledge my worth. Therefore, my destiny is predicated on me understanding the value of my existence.

We view the world through a lens that is molded by our **perspectives**. Our perspectives give birth to our perceptions. But if a camera utilizes multiple lenses, shouldn't we?

I am more than a poet. I am a communicator. In understanding my gift, it is not enough to give you the good, the bad, and the ugly when I write. I must give you everything life has given me and much more. It is through the roads of power, passion, purpose, and perspective, that I allow you to journey with me as I recreate the experiences life has granted me.

Venturing into different styles of poetry, I am transforming myself into an all-around poet. I will leave no stone unturned in this series, as I try my hand at sonnets, haiku's and even a soliloquy. This is only the beginning.

Table of Contents

Power

Black Inception	9
Dear Brotha	12
Endurance	14
History As I Know It	15
How Can I Be Better Than What I'm Seeing	18
I Bet	19
I Cry For The Unsung of The Movement	20
Liz's Boys (English Sonnet)	21
Powerless	22
Stoop Kid	24
The Ghetto Crown Jewel	26
Timelord	28
Typed This One	30

Passion

A Factor of Sex	33
Afflicted Assassin (English Sonnet)	34
Disappointing You (Haiku)	35
Emotional Genocide	36
Facade	37
Hypnotic Hands (English Sonnet)	39
I Hate Buying Flowers	40
Innate (English Sonnet)	41
Instant Karma (Haiku)	42
Laws of Attraction (English Sonnet)	43
Mami	44
Milky Way	45
My Dear Daughters	47
Paradise Lost and Regained	48
Resurrection (Haiku)	49
Suspended Animation	50
That's My Baby	52

The Broken Heart   53
Unsheathe Cupid's Bow (Haiku)   55
Yin and Yang   56

Purpose

Across from me Lies a Graveyard   61
As I Lay Me Down To Sleep   62
Astral Projection   63
Cog's Cognition   64
From the Ilk of Sampson Heracles and Kintaro   65
(English Sonnet)
Healing Energetically through Loving Principles   66
I Jumped (Haiku)   68
I Jumped   69
Philosetry   70
Poseidon's Plea (English Sonnet)   71
The Chosen Ones   72
The Walking Dead   73
What is Fear to the Driven   74

Perspective

10 Months to Nirvana (Italian Sonnet)   77
Anything You Can Do I Can Do Better   78
Artificial Eclipse   79
Burning Sands (English Sonnet)   80
Chicago's Song   81
Chronesthesian Catharsis (English Sonnet)   82
Church Folk   83
Concrete Virus (English Sonnet)   84
Gameplay-Wordplay (English Sonnet)   85
Hero of A Thousand Faces (Soliloquy)   86
I Never Thought   87
Just Scribblin   88
Letter to Daddy   89
Life is I-4   90
Salient Mirror (Haiku)   91

Semantics   92
Siamese Twin   93
Sometimes the Devil is Me (Italian Sonnet)   94
Steal Away   95
Stoic   96
The Paradox of a Servant   97
The Things We Value Most   98
Warrior Personified   99
Yahweh's Letter   101

Power

Black Inception

"Stay woke my brother!"
"Stay woke my sister!"
The words resonated through the atmosphere,
Settling amongst a visceral plane.

"Stay woke my brother!"
"Stay woke my sister!"
Words spoken by sleepwalkers,
With as much power as a conversation
Between street stalkers.
It sounds exciting, yet the value is all the same.

Allow me to separate you
From the sixth floor of your subconscious,
With a question that leaves me nauseous.
Who delivered the Spaniard all of his slaves?

You formed a collective conscience.
Yet, you have an issue that's monstrous.
You refuse to be accountable for your mishaps ...
Inevitably that will prove grave.

One trillion is our expected expenditure budget.
Only two percent of crabs lend support,
While being held by others inside of the bucket.
Self-proclaimed activists ... quick to pass the buck,
You operate under the moniker of Pontius Pilate.

How many know Kirby Puckett?
I'm pushing this narrative viciously,
The ignorance at times engenders me,
It is more than a beverage when I mention Nantucket.
The immediacy stems from the accepted leniency.
Our history is still called Black not American;
Now there's a reason to riot.

I now provide you a series of kicks,
That will initiate a perpetual shift,

To move you through the final five levels
That may have you disheveled.

The fifth floor comprises of fiery eyes.
James Baldwin's notes revolutionized in fifty-five.
This Harlem Renaissance Man's words
Ignited more than pages, the next time that he spoke.

Blood strewn across the fourth floor,
Assassinated before he could turn forty-four,
The driveway was Medgar Evers resting place.
The future was forecasted brightly,
Though it was clouded by gun-smoke.

If confirmation comes in threes,
I need you to remain seated comfortably ...
These last three floors, hold the keys
To an awakening—An allspark.

For some, this may be an epiphany.
Chronicled classics entombed in mystery.
I present you with the rock of our existence—
The matriarch.

I so journeyed for the truth, that has often alluded me.
It is on the third floor, that I'm reminded of 1883 ...
A year where we witnessed
The passing of an abolitionist.

Had to be recognized in 1773,
Her work was measured
Against the finest Shakespearean decrees.
The second floor is an ode
To the West African poet, Phyllis.

The first floor is incredible,
What it holds is indelible.
It was found in the land
Where our **name eternally gave us** substance.

Reaching back with this lineal tentacle,
What I unearthed was irrepressible.
Lucy ... crowned queen of all,
Though some may offer reluctance.

Though I walk through the valley,
Where what appears to be real is not what it seems.
I'm proud of everything that makes me black,
Not shaped by the lucid images of a dream.

Dear Brotha

Dear Brotha,

     I've heard the whispers now turned into full conversations. Black men are finally reaching their destination. The white man's fear is echoed by their representation. I know you feel it in the air. It's an unnerving sensation. They don't want us to win Brotha. We dominate athletics, aesthetics, and we define what is eclectic. We finally made it within despite our color; competing in economics, bionics, and avionics. Our place has been solidified, even though they march and cry. You've seen them running with torches, as if we were Frankenstein. We have to be recognized, through the lens of whomever eyes. Brotha you can finally say, "I have begun to reclaim what's mine." We are winning Brotha. Or are we? Brotha, why is it our women are the chosen people that you demean? I mean, you don't have to like the melanin or her self-reliant regimen. Even if she isn't by your side, her title is still that of a Queen. These accomplishments we have gained thus far, may not be all that they seem. Who's rolling the camera? Who's working the screen? Brotha you are still so angry, but it's misplaced. You are angry with the one person who gets you the most; the person who shares your race. We have come a long way, but have been drawn out in the process. The majority is still in the rear, while the tip of the spear is enjoying the profit. My Brotha, please Brotha, know it was a 300-year-old scheme. Drudged up in 1712, to encapsulate you in a dream. You've become excited with an outhouse, that has been marketed as a penthouse. Yet you have the audacity to mock those that are discovering the real route. This was a setup, to keep you from realizing you could get up. It was designed to keep you focused on facets that looked like change. They knew you wouldn't let up, all they had to do was sit back and let you continually mess up. Your broken will was all that would remain. I know you think this may seem silly, but let me paraphrase a phrase from a similar letter constructed by Willie: Get the strongest nigger you can find. The purest, the surest, the leader among his kind. Bind each body part to the hoof of an equestrian. Then let the beast pull the beast apart; it's sure to bring out the bitch in rest of them. This how you tame the dame that keeps replacing men; you destroy the name they claim and then repeat again.

Brotha the good news is this. They weren't able to cast our history into the abyss. But you have got to stop thinking about the things that don't mean shit. Stocks and equity, not cars and belts. Fuck rocks and celebrity. Let's figure out how to sustain wealth. And I'm not only referring to money Brotha.

Sincerely,

The Truth

Endurance

It is a sorrowful thing,
To have transcendent ideas
Birthed then buried by the children of men.

Still, resist the regime
That rains its rule
Over the physical den.

History As I Know It (I'm Proud To Be Black)

I need you to be proud of who you are,
For better or worse—evermore
Stand on the scars you have caused and earned;
Bring to the table issues that people yearn ...
Let them seep through History's pores.

In 1896, Gandhi was a man of non-violence
And withstanding pressure.
Demanded the relevance of Indians,
But wouldn't dine with the Kaffers.
Who knew this high-souled sage was an illusionist?
Have to admit it was clever.
Behind that disarming gaze,
Laid a man who considered us niggers.

In the orient lays a land,
Laden with lessons and arts that can rapture.
Boasting a wall infused with the epidermis
Of customs and culture.
At night, the aroma of gunpowder
Blankets the rafters.
By day, the golden children in Tiananmen
Are surrounded by vultures.

Land of the free—
We've labeled these United States.
Conquering and establishing a footprint,
Was always her fate.
Stand in awe of how you defeated the British,
Move after move placing them in checkmate.
However, never forget how we claim the Native
Americans as family;
Yet disrespect them every November
By dining with turkeys on our plates.
How should they react?
Should they participate?
Or should they have the partitioned piece of property
We so graciously gave back, in order to celebrate?

Now let me take a snapshot from two pieces of time.
To give an audience to black legends,
Who were optimal in their prime:

The gravity of the situation was unearthed by Newton.
So, after he was assassinated,
Could you keep his people from rioting and looting?
Taken—because he wasn't in your conglomerate.
When's the last time you've seen some labeled
a terrorist, holding a doctorate.

In the 2000's plot, K Dot saw an unsavory narrative
Trying to deplete us.
So, when he said Negus, it was in order to feed us;
That truth that we so desperately reinvent and ignore.
From the home of royal courts,
Came rolling tombs over rumbling seas—
Enthralled by years of dis-ease.
Arranged puzzle pieces strewn under a wooden floor.

And before you tell me about Black Lives Matter
And how the Panthers became perverted,
Trust me I'm well aware of my people.
I appreciate all of your concern
And efforts that were concerted,
Let me take care of my people.

Some of you claim to be a part of the unsung,
Yet you feed the insatiable beast we call perception.
I didn't forget about you,
You're my honorable mention.
You are just as divisive,
As the enemies you say deal in deception.
If you want to operate with effectiveness,
You need only to look at past abolitionists
And true activists during their inception.

I am proud to be black;
You who look like me, please do not muddy it.
I am proud to be black;

You who are curious about me, I invite you to study it.

Carry the burden;
Let the knowledge acknowledge
What you have done and still do.
Allow me to revel in my version,
As you celebrate your absolute truth.

How Can I Be Better Than What I'm Seeing

How can I be better than what I'm seeing?
Working all day, and they ain't hardly eating.
No one to invest or trust in what they believe in;
Started another cycle, the last didn't complete em.

How can I be better than what I'm seeing?
Boys, believing being hood is some holy credence.
Girls exploited ... it's only attention they're seeking.
Misguided guidance; how can I not be seething?

How can I inspire an entire nation?
The truth is I don't want to inspire,
But be an example for you to face
Those things you are already facing.
Have the courage to pursue
Those things you were told to quit chasing;
Realize the power in your purpose,
Out of the wasteland where you have been wasting.

How do I encourage myself to keep on moving?
The weight of my vision at times I can bear,
Other times so unbridled and so un-soothing.
All of this inclusion, negativity, and disapproving;
I feel like I'm imbued with the conscious of past souls,
Where concepts of life began improving.
They cry out ...
Wanting to remind us of what it was like to be human.
When success wasn't based on acumen, aesthetics,
Winning, or losing.

How can I be better than what I'm seeing?
I'm trying to be better ... trying to clot the bleeding.
One step at a time, one foot on the line;
Disburden myself from fearful and false heedings.
Push on with the fight, keep on proceeding.

I Bet

I bet you think I'm that trader.
That Uncle Tom,
That would say anything to get a favor.

I bet you think I'm that token.
The savior of his kind.
The one who wasn't broken.

I bet you think I forgot
Where I came from.
The nights of gun shots;
The sounds of false freedom.

I bet you think I put on for you.
That I "speak proper",
In order to acclimate to what you do.

I bet that you are still mesmerized.
This is no illusion.
People from where I am from
Can deduce, and provide intellectual conclusions.

I bet you have no idea
What to do with me.
Here's a start.
Have a conversation.
Don't assume foolishly.

I Cry for The Unsung of The Movement

I cry for those not known in the annals of history as activists.
I cry for the countless slain on the streets paved with gold.
I cry for the mothers, the fathers, the daughters,
and the sons—the advocates.
I cry for the thousands that marched ...
the meek, the poor, the sick, the young, and the old.
I cry for the multitude who were beaten for living the constitution,
and were labeled as terrorists.
I cry for those whose fire they tried to drench with a hose.
I cry for the many who were herded like cattle,
exposed to the crackle of a prod, though they were pacifists.
Oh Lord, cries my soul.

My tears shed for Viola, for Medgar, for Hosea, and for Malcolm.
My tears shed for Rosa, for Emmett,
for too many whose horrors I couldn't fathom.
My tears shed for the stagnation of a people,
whose legacy is storied in chasms.
But I will dry these tears, my resolve won't sear,
I am emboldened by my ancestral phantoms.

Liz's Boys

Legasey, will peer where the eye can't go.
His thoughts, guided by elite intellect.
T's lens crafts a perspective that will show—
Contagious laugh, combined with etiquette.
M dot; sovereign creative wizardry.
Erecting life, from vocals and a pen.
Pushing through stern obstacles, valiantly;
Ceo's destiny—already written.
From my center porch, I am on the verge ...
Of a stage, to host my kinsmen's talents.
This tethered realization I purge.
Cut from the cloth, of a selfless parent.
Brothers—no luckier sibling than I;
The world has birthed a new impactful five.

Powerless

Re-appropriation: words that used to be derogatory,
Gaining accepted use by usually oppressed people.
This is its truth, no mystic allegory.
Transformed into a positive reform—absolved of evil.

To my forefathers and foremothers,
I mean no disrespect.
But I refuse, to let them misuse and retool—
Our history, for their cause and effect.

Provided was an often-overlooked definition.
Never really brought up, in a topic of contention.
 "Experts" suggest, we have damaged our children.
Before I forget to mention this question ...
Why is it, you try to re-appropriate
Our re-appropriation to fit your divisive incisions?

I see it.
How to try to promulgate your narratives.
Permeating our thoughts, in order to revisit—
The pain, the suffering, the obstacles and challenges.

Nice try.
How about our victories
And future accomplishments?
And continue to listen, before you ask why.
Did you know nigga is a derivative
From a different continent?

That's right—
Negus ... and this isn't the poem to render its meaning.
Another day, for another fight.
Shout out to Kendrick for the insight he was gleaning.

Oh, let's not forget about the host of pejorative words;
I did a little gold mining.
Like how you still say gook and jap.
Ummm, those need some refining.

Wait, there's more buddy.
They're called Native Americans;
Not Indians, you dummy.
Adjust the compass, according to the facts.
In fact, you call a spic a wetback.
I'm trying to figure out, what country is that?
I mean, Spain is European and Mexico is Hispanic.
After everything, are you still going to allow him
To sail the wrong way—into the Atlantic?

Now you've got the denial face on ...
Muttering words like antics—and—he's just kidding.
Only semantics.
Let me channel my inner Westbrook ...
"What?"
You still don't get it, dammit.
I feel like I'm the alien, among Martians—
On their own fucking planet.

I know ... That was quite a robust explanation.
But, for those that feed off of the negative connotation,
Which you try to place on my new word,
My pronoun, my designation ...

When I see you, you will be the first ones I address.
To deepen your understanding,
That your view of our word nigga—is POWERLESS.

Stoop Kid

Dis nigga's wildin'—
Look at him always stylin'.
In dem books grindin'.
Backpack too heavy—
What fuckin' mountain is he climbin'?

Dis nigga's wildin'—
The Chinese nigga,
With all his computations and equations.
Only homogenous relations.
Never an object of deportation?
Those sidewalk sales ain't causin' inflation?

Dees nigga's wildin'—
Ayo, look at these Arab and Indian niggas.
How many hotels they own?
They not even homegrown ... my nigga.
And with all these changes,
I wouldn't be so quick to set anything in stone—
My nigga ... If I was them.

Dis nigga's wildin'—
Papi you stay at the corner store.
Matter fact, where's dem boriquas I saw.
You keep makin' butter rolls; selling lottery tickets
And Kung Fu condoms.
Hold down that inventory shit,
I'm lookin' for dem bori—
Neva mind Papi, I found em.
Papi wildin' my nigga.

Ha-haaaa.
And this white nigga; Casper the friendly ghost.
Every time I see him, he's makin' a toast.
Daddy left him that empire,
Nigga always doin' the most.
Life for him consists of stocks, bonds, cars,
Trips, weddins', school, privilege—all this variety—

Fuckin' receptionist host.

My nigga ...
What are you talkin' 'bout?
You're the one that's buggin'.
You've been on the stoop, 30 years ... ain't do nothin'.
You observe all of their success and live in fear—
Keep on fussin'.
I know ... you must be waitin' on somethin'?

Dis—nigga—is wildin'.
Here comes Martin in all his glory and writin'.
Keep an eye out for Huey,
There's sure to be some protests and riotin'.
And ole Detroit, Malcolm executed by his own, Red.
Nigga who made you the reincarnation of Christ? N',
Who made you the spokesperson for us? You triflin'.
Who the fuck is you—my nigga?

My nigga ... I'm you.
If you would be still, steel yourself, and quit fightin'.
I'm your ultimate draft you've,
In secret, been designin'.
It's facts my nigga ...
I'm you.

The Ghetto Crown Jewel

I am hood!

I did not misspeak—
I am **h**onor,
optimism,
overachievement, and
determination.
Hope to the hopeless;
offering
overarching,
dedication.

At the mention of this fact,
How is it that you
overreact—with
obscure
delusions?
Howling,
obsessively;
overt
diffusion.

With phrases like:
"That is **h**orrible,
obscene,
offensive, and
derogatory."
"**H**ostile word—
only
option Webster's
depository.

How unfortunate. What you fail to realize, is—
I was forged in **h**urt,
oppression,
opacity, and
depression.
Hurled into an

oblique,
offkey,
derision.

Now a phoenix reborn of
Humble,
ordered,
organic
dimensions.
Proud to be free—and no longer
heed, an
obscure,
obtrusive,
detention.

Timelord (His-Story Part 2)

I saw the past, the present, the future,
and was incensed.
Enchanted by the sweet aroma of progression,
yet vexed by the stench of regression;
in the same instance.

I was enchanted by the sweet aroma of progression.
Yet perplexed by the stench of regression.
Floating through the annals of time,
sifting through every thought, every lesson.
I had to step back from this wary ascension.
Time is ever fleeting and there's too much to mention.

I saw the past pushing past the future,
to regain a strong-hold.
Enslaving us with the same tools
that they made them hold.
Digital chains, whips, and picks—
flash flood media to stain our souls.
How long is his story going to be replayed,
but remain untold?

His story doesn't repeat itself.
It never really ended.
Like the volumes on a shelf,
the tale continuously gets extended.
Characters alter names, start new journeys,
some facts even get amended—
And when the conclusion comes close,
here's the spinoff, just like the author intended.

Through all phases of time,
There was one constant enemy.
Through the past, present, and future,
they always fought an inner me.
That bore false facts, false hopes,
and created a synergy.

Which caused blindness,
and let them stumble aimlessly.

So now I face that enemy without hesitation.
I do battle with that inner me,
with all conviction and condemnation.
I operate on faith not fear,
and press forward to my destination.
And when I get there,
take others with me to partake in this celebration.

They are my past, you are my present,
we are our future.

Typed This One

I usually would write a little some'
Or record a few puns.
But in the spirt of fun,
Ima type this one.

So I opened up a computer screen,
To see what would happen.
What resulted was 5 years of cryptic inaction.
Unshacklin' the Obelisk, only a fraction.
Nothin' can stop these empirical pistols from clappin'.

Let you tap into my conscious, 'til my soul's siphoned.
Impartin' you with these gifts,
That's got my whole enlightened.
Ctrl, Alt, Del any negatives—
I swear my senses heightened.
The proof is in the proverbs
Of these .docs I'm scribin'.

Can't backspace all those decisions;
They're already in motion.
Alt tabbin' frequently through the past,
Looking for somethin' to hope in.
Page downin' through the process;
The pain's too much it's hurtin'.
It's smoothenin' out that diamond—
My guarantee is certain.

And with the faith of a mustard seed ...
I enchant these keys;
To record prophecies—
For my implanted trees.

Though I usually would write a little some'...
Pages drunk with metaphors,
Enough to stir a convent of nuns.
This was more than a spirit of fun—I had to type this one.

Passion

A Factor of Sex

In the opening session,
You fell victim to 1 of my charms.
Royal preparation for this lesson;
Seated at the throne of a king, disrobed and disarmed.

That feeling is intoxicating,
When the 7th spot is accessed by 14 angles,
The experience is twice as exhilarating,
Watching you become drunk with ecstasy,
Vines entangled.

For 21 minutes, I would have been bitten
At least 7 times;
In 3 different instances.
Nails dug into my back,
As I grind through the thighs that bind.
Pain becomes pleasure's craved antithesis.

Raised above my head,
I gave you 5 minutes of overcast clarity.
After moving you from the wall to the bed,
The tremors in both legs forecasted
The 10-minute storm that showered me.

I would give up 4 lifetimes,
To replay all of this again.
The fact is, what I have come to find ...
Is this isn't sex, but an epiphany,
When you enter my den.

Afflicted Assassin

Athenic complex; Apollo structure.
The house was built along twenty fortnights.
The first encounter; barrier ruptured.
A surreptitious blow begins the blight.
Disguised as courtship; only enchantment.
Cur'sed genes encoded by Romulus.
Designed illusion of shared entrapment—
Unknowing shadow of an Incubus.
Subverted conscious premeditation.
Destined; Is destiny—the enemy.
This gift defines altered divination.
No stars are crossed, in this epiphany.
Lamenting—There isn't a scroll chiller.
The hidden memoir of a heart killer.

Disappointing You

It is subconscious.
I disrupt nature's balance.
You leave, I suffer.

Emotional Genocide

You didn't allow me to be buried peacefully,
Resurrecting me too early from the grave.
I was still a corpse, mummified easily.
What about any of this, should be considered brave?

The subtle attacks ...
Scratching, scraping, scathing my being.
Numerous abrasions, turned into lacerations,
Wounding this wolf—wailing silently.
Consumed by your anger,
Shrouded by the crimson veil of unseeing ...
Vengeance coddles the urn,
That is stirred violently.

I understand you are scorched,
And need some venting.
Yet, searing my image
Will turn my flesh to stone.
The folly is in your excoriating message—
It's unrelenting.
The knives, you don't realize you're inserting,
Will soon have no home.

Gravely wounded once before,
I have managed to recover a piece of myself
In the midst of this circumstance.
Before you set the stage, to close all doors,
Know somethings once broken ...
Never get a second chance.

Facade

America consumes 80% of the world's illicit drugs.
People escaping from trauma
By plunging into an alternate reality.
I can't judge them though ...
Perhaps laughter is my drug of choice.
You don't know my pain because of the phalanx
Of smiles I produce to shield it.

Yes, when we are together my joy is pure
And my revelry is true.
But when I'm without you,
I laugh to keep from imagining the feeling
Of your head nestled against my chest.
I laugh to keep from sensing
Your touch along the contours of my skin.

They know my strength through resiliency.
I know my weakness through reliance.
Alone, I am left with a selection of thoughts
That solder my solitude.

Not depression, but a self-reflection:
A reflection on the things I have said
To make you unsure at times.
A reflection of the way you smile,
That paralyzes time itself.
A reflection of the fact that our arguments
Are not because we despise each other,
But because we love each other so much ...

So much, that the pain apart—
Is worse than dying.
And the circumstances we are in make "us"
A difficult thing when it shouldn't be.
The fact that men shouldn't cry is a lie.
Look at the streams of dried salt that stain my face.
They are the tributaries of my story.

Tomorrow I will laugh again.
You won't know that tonight was torture without you.
They won't know that I am weak without you.
I am so strong, but I am beginning to become tired.
I know I don't let you see it.
But I need you.

Hypnotic Hands

Fingers interlaced in hair follicles,
Wrapped around my wrist, they pull as I thrust.
Pressure ensures pleasure is optimal.
Achieving an orgasm is a must.
Caress the sternum outlining your chest.
Gently trace the path from stomach to hips.
This is your brief respite; instance of rest.
Your moment is coming, don't tame the drip.
Opened by my thumbs; prepare for entry.
Saliva falls from my tongue and ... bullseye.
Unlock your gates—I am the lone sentry.
Receive this message my touch does not lie.
Whispers in your ears locks you in my land.
Witness the dance of my hypnotic hands.

I Hate Buying Flowers

I hate buying real flowers.
They die.
I like the plastic ones;
Those are the kind, only once you have to buy.

The thought of romance,
Disappeared when my heart was frozen.
True affection had a limited advance,
To whomever filled the role that was chosen.

But then we stumbled across each other.
A path was woven by the fates of destiny.
You unlocked the emotions I smothered;
It was inevitable that I regained the rest of me.

Now, I look at plastic flowers differently.
They remind me of a truth that lacks consistency.
Behind closed doors,
The facade is no more than a contingency.

Take a real flower—The Rose.
It was meant to cease.
Like passion and affection that wanes and grows;
They need rekindling, under and outside of the sheets.

Symbolic like a Rose,
Our time together has been organic.
I can no longer suppress the thoughts that arose.
The word Love, no longer causes me to panic.

I used to hate buying real flowers,
Because they'd die.
Now, I can't wait to buy them.
And you're the reason why.

Innate

No words can account for this emotion.
Lost in a world of wanting and needing.
Strong cues of non-verbal, for this notion.
What has been brewing will soon be seething.
There is no defeating this sensation.
You can't hide the symptoms that manifest.
Immense longing and sleep deprivation,
Lay siege in whichever place you take rest.
This thing I speak of, is seen in old tales.
The imperfect perfection ... trust is true.
Though it seems you have searched to no avail,
Someone was created that reflects you.
Allowing my soul to merge with this mate,
This feeling ... only described as innate.

Instant Karma

I accept the pain.
Absence makes me love you more.
This breeds loneliness.

Laws of Attraction

Lonely path; I wasn't in sight of you.
Seamless vulnerability displayed.
You recognized the same in you, was true.
Drawn, yet scared to push each other away.
Unaware of our reflection, at first.
Undressed our souls in the fogless mirror—
No relief from this insatiable thirst.
Fingers trace cloned scars, that we discover.
We orbit, as you search my orbital.
Feast on me, distill this vacant presence.
Witness your sage—revere my oracle.
You can't drain me; behold your twin essence.
Acknowledging the worst that can happen,
Opposites don't mesh ... Laws of Attraction.

Mami

¿Que tu hace?
She responds. "Lo que tu no hace."
I tell her, "Whoa! Mas o menos."
"I speak Spanish in pieces and pebbles."

I ask her, "Why you stare at me?"
"Why you even laughing doe?"
She licks her lips, then shifts her hips
And whispers, "Papi DIMELO!"

Whether it's her sensual salsa
Or keeping me in rhythm during bachata,
Let me get a taste
I know she's sweeter than horchata.

I ask her, "How we get in here?"
"Is this really what you want Ma?"
She licks her lips, before we kiss
She whispers, "Papi TOMA!"

Milky Way

Temporal and spatial suspension,
Lock clocks.
There's only time to feast,
On this astrological crockpot:

Synaptic conquest—
Ready for war I air these.
Laid them out one by one on the table,
In Pisces.

Scorched my opinion of this oasis.
Paralyzed by the serum of your mirage.
This epiphany has torn us from our past shells,
With a bludgeoning barrage.

If I can answer all of your questions,
Would you allow me in your court?
Embrace this confrontation—
And forego the chains around your fort.

I'm curious.
Is it she or us,
That has this tidal essence sealed …
8 trigrams palmed lotus.

My sage told us she was mythical,
But my spells disarm.
And for the night cap hind strap,
Ring the horn.

Pastellic, mosaic, perfection—sun setting reflection—
Should I admire who?
I pray you don't consume me—
Before I devour you.

Liberate my id,
With impartial ecstasy.
Engulf this dull sarcophagus,

With distilled dichotomy.

Stripped of all layers.
Exposed our clay …
My primordial instincts,
Transcend your Milky Way.

My Dear Daughters

I cannot describe the emotion, through penmanship,
That has possessed my thoughts of you two.
It surpasses joy and happiness ...
A plane of existence that operates beyond time.

Thank you for being the essence of me
That will invigorate the future.
My dear daughters,
Take the best of me and share it with the world.
You are the legacy that was written
When I was conceived.
I love you.

Paradise Lost and Regained

The instant it hit him,
The realization must have felt like something new.
Similar to voyagers following their compass;
Seeing distortions forming in the horizon's view.

Your first time riding a bicycle,
Without the two bolted anchors ...
That first kiss on your quivering lips,
In exchange of the usual banter.

Nostrils itching at the mixture
Of Spring condensation and Earth,
Emanating from Central Park's grass—
Experiencing your first maelstrom of a hailstorm,
Sensing the lightning and thunder clash.

That feeling which steals the essence of life,
Floating in your lungs.
The last note in a symphony,
When the harpsicord is strung.

He knew that feeling well enough.
This opportunity would never again seem true.
So, he captured this moment.
Which was all he could do ...

When he was once again able to see you.

Resurrection

Unearth this pink husk.
Buried beneath the damp soil ...
Parts of our tinder.

Suspended Animation

If the stars could realign,
you would have your own constellation.
The ocean would separate waves,
the jungle come alive with elation.
Every step you take,
would force the earth to exhibit another sensation.
The thought of you has me in suspended animation.

Unlocking my conscious,
exploring pathways I have never before.
Releasing emotions, confirming every notion,
shaking my being to its very core.
The heart agrees with the mind,
as it pumps blood into all chambers; four.
It's the all-encompassing you,
the holistic person that I adore.

This is what it feels like,
when you're caught up by surprise.
Peering deep into the soul,
reflecting off the mirrors in your eyes.
Creating dreams, creating visions, creating bonds,
solidifying ties—
Unwavering, unfaltering, these concepts I realize.
I'll go a little further, sit back and analyze.

I can't shift this connection.
Past feeling to this, not to my recollection;
Words like gorgeous, reliable, of course perfection,
Flow from my synapse without pause or hesitation.

I'll make it perfectly clear ...
Because you love people like you do,
Smile gracious, and ensue—
To be determined, to be ambitious,
to be enduring and pull through;
This ailment has got a hold of me like the flu.

But I'll stand still for this moment,
for this snapshot in time, for this view.
I'll get enveloped in this instance.
I'll stay in awe of you.

That's My Baby

They don't make any like this one,
Because she was made for me.
Shares my attributes of seriousness,
But can be just as goofy.
Ambitious of what will come,
Where others refuse to see.
Yet, will take time to let time pass with me ...
Lost in the stars ... on a rooftop like Snoopy.

Y'all still looking for Bonnie—
I have Mrs. Clyde.
She allows me to be Dr. Jekyl in public,
And in the bedroom—Mr. Hyde.
Swept away my past with the broomstick,
That she will jump over to be my bride.
This princess has become another piece,
To the puzzle that is my pride.

Oh yes, she's my kind of crazy.
No need to fill you in on too much,
That's between me and my lady.
A rock who holds me down when others are hazy.
I never get tired of saying it, that's my baby.

The Broken Heart

The catatonic look in your eyes
Reveals much about your soul.
A look that says I do not understand
The pain you are feeling.
A pain that has morphed from emotional to physical.
Attacking the very thing I swore to protect—

A piercing feeling ...
As if an invisible knife lies in wait,
Through every choice I make—
That doesn't include you.
A knife that nurses you to sleep every night;

The bed side companion I no longer am.

A feeling that causes you to claw at your chest,
Separating the skin in order to remove the blade—
From what is left in your reservoir.
You think I don't know what it feels like,
But you are mistaken.
You introduced me to this painful process
Years ago,
Staunching the flames of my creativity,
Staunching the essence of my awakening,
Entrapping me within me.

Yet—
I will never hate you.
For there are times I hate myself for hurting you.
But I cannot live in false happiness.
I can no longer appease the thoughts of others.
I am apathetic to their advice and yours.
I can no longer mend the strands of your broken heart.

Once a slave to my own shattered chambers.
I became a slave to yours.
But—
I have purged myself of my penance.

Find your freedom in the fires of rebirth.
If you don't,
You will fall victim
To a reality of days past.

Unsheathe Cupids Bow

I always miss you;
The moment your lips leave mine.
Lift my soul again.

Yin and Yang

Very similar, yet different ...
That in essence is the title of this poem's sentiment.
The truth about you being heaven sent,
Is at times imbedded in our arguments.

Never has there been a woman to capture my attention,
Making everything feel so new.
Exposing my flaws—
Allowing me to reassess my inner who.

One who can laugh with me from dawn
Until dusk is through.
And is a walking simile
Of everything I do.

But with all we have in common,
There lingers a recurring problem ...
At times, my approach has been too solemn—
In the ways of before.
We trudge through territory that is foreign.
The soil that we are trying to toil,
Becomes unstable when storms pour in.
Acknowledging our differences is how we
Are going to unlock the door.

You see Yin chases Yang forever.
A promise they made to each other,
When they decided to be together.
And it is shown by the dots that are tethered ...
Behind them as a symbolic gesture.

In those dots are varying thoughts.
In those dots are battles to be fought.
In those dots are experiences that can't be taught.
In those dots lie revelations that are often sought.

I've always admired those two for their pursuit.
Unconditional is the word that strengthens the root.

They never asked to be perfect, only ripened fruit.
I use them as our constant, iconic proof.

Purpose

Across from me Lies a Graveyard

A young child adorned in cotton and denim,
Plays as the grass sways
In the lifeless breeze.
The mother kneels in silence, in solace,
In open solitude to remember ...
Eerie is the plot of marble tombs
And broken headstones—
Eerie not because of the tales
Of apparitions that accompany it.
Eerie not because of the Cherubs
That stand guard by day,
Yet move at night.
Eerie not because of the wildlife
That joins in the evening chorus without fail.
Eerie because ... the mother
Is asking the unspoken question,
As she peers into the beginning—dash—end.
The thought that looms in the fog of her memory,
Just as it does in the skirt of the sky—
Did he die achieving everything?
Or did another destiny fertilize the flowers of pain
And unkempt promises?

As I Lay Me Down To Sleep

As I lay on this man-made bosom of comfort,
I can't help but be enticed by the flittering images
That taunt me as I doze in and out of freedom.
Furthermore, the prospect of a lucid interview
Is one that demands my utmost attention.
I can't control this nocturnal
Plane of existence.
Every subtle jerk of my body,
To influence this world of hope and horror,
Is predetermined.
When I awake, I will not remember all
That has taken place.
The irony is that a dream resembles
My conscious state.
Am I asleep while living?

Astral Projection

I sense that this feeling is uncanny.
Not the frightening recognition of déjà vu,
But the eerie knowing that it was coming.
It, being my ability to see myself outside of my life.
Life, moving in 4D.
Insomuch that every choice is linear,
Yet perpendicular.
Choices that appear to be mine, yet omniscient.
Decisions that are out of my hands,
Yet held firm in them—
No mid-life crisis but an awakening,
From a cryogenic state of dependence
On another's dream.
As I thaw,
The pain from the frostbite of wasted time lingers.
I see now ...
It wasn't time that you stole.
It was a false projection you provided.

Cog's Cognition

Watchmaker: Little cog who told you,
you were the smallest of gears.

Cog: Watchmaker I am.
They said so themselves.
I've been a small piece to the puzzle,
All of these years.

Watchmaker: Cog look at your grooves,
The spurs from being spurned are unique.
You are like no other.

Cog: But they said I was the same;
Of no different name.
They welcomed me as their brother.

Watchmaker: Dear little gear.
If only you'd hear.
The words I speak to you.
You were never a part,
From the very start.
Don't let them take that too.

Cog: Watchmaker ...
I'm confused as to the words you say.
I am comfortable where I exist.
If I leave now,
My absence will cause a rift.

Watchmaker: You need only to look
Outside of the glass
That has reflected the internal workings.
Your design can move any machine;
Simple or complex I'm certain.

From the Ilk of Sampson, Heracles, and Kintaro

Cur'sed blessing is this day to be born,
Among the praise of God and human tongue.
Though scrolls of past give heed and often warn,
Fate's sepulchre was made to woo the young.
Plagued by the need to purge the battlefield,
Of vessels ... that are purposed to be foes.
Adorned with brute strength or a brazen shield;
Gifts for the lot of those who have been chose.
Wondrous to be hailed as part deity.
Tales tell of the victories I have claimed.
Each slain, takes a piece of humanity—
Steep price to be paid to record a name.
Rest on my back the warrior's mantle.
With a piercing blade and crimson handle.

Healing Energetically through Loving Principles

I'm staring at my past and my future—
The mixture is making the present murky.
Unstated is the state of this culture.
I peer into the eyes of vessels,
That are the rebirthed me.

They say no quid pro quo,
But it's quid pro show.
Liabilities, policies, and bureaucracies;
Fail those who are left
To tend with unfacilitated faculties.
I feel like the reincarnation of Socrates.
Why produce all of these fallacies?

False stories and false prophets;
Focused to stack their wallets.
Meanwhile, the chosen sit in solace ...
In solitude, in ineptitude—but they're the multitude.
What are they supposed to do; when you won't do
What you're supposed to do?

And when their souls shake,
The earth quakes.
But your eyes are too high to see it ...
Floating on elevated platforms,
The burden you already conceded.
Looking down on the ants you've labeled defeated.
I watered their grass; it's already seeded.
Watch them grow from their past.
I've already seen it.

Just let me help.
Like I need to help.
Like I'm supposed to help.
You waste and wait.
I'm strapped up, boots laced, clasped my belt.
Let me change them—save them.
Their hell is real, but the heaven's felt.

If you won't abide by the principles you claim,
I'll take up the mantle
Until they can find the value in their name.

I Jumped

I jumped, no reserve.
It was already in flight.
Orange sky, new eyes.

I Jumped

I jumped, no reserve;
Saw 10,000 falling.
Looked up, counted to 5;
Saw 10,000 calling.
Saw mine; met it with a smile,
Then started sprawling.
Pop cord, no discord;
Stood up—got to hauling.

Philosetry

The fear of moving forward,
Is like being afraid of bait in a can.
It is like the hysterical thoughts
That prevent you from moving toward ...
The great catch hidden offshore of land.

It is like being in a club dancing,
When you spot the one you wish to hold.
Yet, rejection keeps you from advancing.
But you will never date destiny,
If every hand you've drawn you fold.

If I stand still and never pursue,
I will never capture my game.
If I hunt, until my energy can't be renewed;
All in all, my existence is still the same.

Poseidon's Plea

It was the fall of twelve that gave man thought;
His quest for significance internal.
In time, battles over ideals were fought,
Dampening the source that was eternal.
Thus, the journey of immortal and man
Became a course pilfered by the wayward.
Throughout decades, the tug of war was span.
Oft the path should lean fore, but is starboard.
The quad beast's wail, accompanied by death,
Thrashes above the oceanic floor.
It calls to the ear of wandering breath,
And spurns the relic that is human spoor.
Dire letters in spouts and hurricanes.
Atlantis ... where inanimate dreams wane.

The Chosen Ones

This is what it is to be a broken home …
Tattered lines, connect the phone …
Wicked white noise, is all that's known—
Jungle dawn, bastard fawn, left alone.

No test, without a testament.
You can't teach without being a student.
Beaten down by the rude and prude,
Made you prudent.
They ran from their destiny—you shouldn't.

The Chosen Ones.

The Walking Dead

It was a tale in two cities,
That held the antidote to my zombie-like state.
Latching on to the dreams of others ...
Asleep yet thinking I was awake.

Here! Catch this serum,
For the virus that has infected you.
The progenitor of this systemic venom,
Is generous in misdirecting you.

A population engendered by listless rhetoric,
And guided by misplaced confidence.
A comfortable collective—
You label the visionaries as heretics;
Clouding the truth, has risen in society's prominence.

The sedative known as fear,
Has been enough to create slaves.
Images and thoughts that may never appear,
Paralyze the populace making aspirations concave.

In this arid wasteland
Of hemmed hopes and brittle choices,
I have found the courage to withstand
The silent beast that quells our voices.

What is Fear to The Driven?

What is fear to the Driven?
Just a mocked-up legend;
Prompting the mass to run
Away from life's many lessons.
A phantom that was born out of abstract tension.
The opposite of faith—pure apprehension.

What is fear to the Driven?
It's a tell-tale dream.
Weaving its seeds into the fabric
Of a great man's seams.
Stagnation is the proclamation;
We know its scheme.
Fake news if you will,
If you know what I mean.

What is fear to the Driven?
Only a concept that was risen,
From peers who wouldn't dare
Push on with decisions.
To move forward when it came to a vision—
Defeated before the process
Began to plan out a mission.

What is fear to the Driven?
It is absolutely nothing.
An intangible thought,
That lives to be something.
But it dies every day to all that's becoming ...
By the hands and feet of visionaries
That keep on running.

Perspective

10 Months to Nirvana

You have been the epitome of me,
Gleaning from my nuance and direction.
Discovered a consummate reflection;
You are the doppelganger that I see.
Resolve; the strength of a Sequoia tree.
Mirrored my keen sense of observation.
Some wish for a son, of reconstruction.
You are what I expected you to be.
Formed in the culvert of forty-four weeks,
Soon overwhelmed, the emotions were rife.
Just to witness my reincarnation ...
From your inception, guarding you when meek—
Watching you grow, for the rest of your life,
Will cut off my Samsara's formation.

Anything You Can Do I Can Do Better

Facebook—Twitter—Snapchat and Insta,
Will never be revered
Like Abraham, Ishmael, and Krishna.
Buddha, beads, chant, Ohmmmmm,
Offerings to Shiva;
Put the money in, turn the dial;
Watch it fall out the dispensa.

Si-mi-lar mess-a-ges:
Uplift the moral and ethical,
Survive the tests and the testaments,
Discard the nonessential and septical.

Yet with all that praising—and all that prose,
I still don't like you, because of what you've chose.

Artificial Eclipse

The day was August 21st.
The film in the atmosphere was opaque ...
The eclipse was coming.
Across the country bonds were forged
In the flames of oneness.
The river of tears
Broke the dams of separation.
This feels like America.

Today is August 28th.
The film in the atmosphere is opaque ...
No eclipse is coming.
Across the country prejudice still looms,
In the gallows of cities, towns, and pastures.
Unity has been untied.
And the walls separate us once again.
This feels like America.

Burning Sands

The first group session masked uncertainty.
Except to expect, the unexpect yet—
Decisions loom of quitting, possibly…
Our will, will show resolve when it is met.
Spectators, oblivious to the show;
Vague eyes, hazy rules, shatter lassiez-faire.
Held accountable for what we don't know,
Repent—across an equidistant square.
All abject faces search for answers still.
Promise of a brotherhood, is our boon.
Synchronized voices echo the oak's shrill—
Gazing left … clasp to the light of the moon.
Deep thoughts of days and nights when we locked hands;
Never lost—traversing the burning sands.

Chicago's Song

We were never taught your ideals.
Some shown to us, others we created.
Didn't have the tools to cope
With the emotions we would feel,
We were oblivious,
But you knew what was already anticipated.

Solve the same problem,
With old solutions—that's insanity.
Dissolving the foundation, crippling the community.
You've already taken my humanity.
Now take away my felonies; give me an opportunity.

We got ladders, but no roofers.
Give me a real profession.
Out of survival, we raise shooters.
Escaping from reality, we go to another dimension.

Without guidance, we are primordial—
Killing and fighting is sensible.
No paths set by tangible sages or oracles.
Vengeance has become our principle.

Isn't this what animals do?
Acting normal for our conditions.
A little uneasy, when exposed to the truth ...
We caution you to listen; put us in a better position.

So every night you will hear our song
Echoing through the alleys,
Until you give us different instruments
To express what we have suppressed.
Our dead will continue to fill up the valleys ...
If you aren't brave enough to care,
Why should we do our best?

Chronesthesian Catharsis

Reflecting on days when I was younger,
I encounter a storied memory:
The yearning for wisdom that grew stronger.
Those moments I covet like ivory.
Approaching the era of middle years,
My focus has shifted to clear visions.
The course of my life I earnestly steer,
To ensure my seeds have their provisions.
A foreign future captivates my thoughts.
A place where serenity rests in kind.
Where accomplishments are no longer sought,
Save a tranquil and a familial mind.
After I have placed everything in line,
I wonder ... can one really measure time?

Church Folk

He can prophesy.
She's an evangelist.
They speak in tongues.

He can discern.
She's healed the sick.
They move people with words sung.

I gave a homeless man a dollar,
Where not one of them could see.
They won't know about it,
When they see me in church.
Isn't that how it should be?

Concrete Virus

The quest for success is marginalized.
Creating a world ideal for the hood.
Choices made that are often penalized,
By tenants of a house misunderstood.
Girls professing themselves to be women;
Clinging to the facade of a father.
Gifting what should be held for the chosen,
Stark loneliness is her story's author.
Achievement is measured in the primal,
For those boys birthed into this arid land.
Bred in contempt—authority's rival,
Must survive by any means that he can.
Time is measured in seconds on their clocks.
Avoiding the pains of life in bagged rocks.

Gameplay/Wordplay

I don't know what all the fuss is about.
The arts nowadays, leave less thought than doubt.
Games focus their attention on graphics.
Lyrics—lack luster exchanged for antics.
The seeds from Wale, Nas, Kendrick, and Kane ...
Hours lost to Mario, just ain't the same.
When did it become all about pixels?
No longer musicians—daft visuals.
Embalmed by the lure of inane false chords;
Only to climb on top of leaderboards.
Though vagrance seeks to leech on every node,
Substance resounds in this forgotten ode.
I will not conform, nor will I astray.
Give me the 90's deft, and game-word play.

Hero of A Thousand Faces

As I embark on this soliloquy, this labyrinth of truths; truths
wrapped in ideals; ideals guided by my perception—Well ... my
perception is guided by my ideals, which are warped by my truths.
Producing a labyrinth of introspection—I can't help but posit: Is this
a fusion of William and Langston? Never mind the introduction;
merely loose words spurred from the idea of soliloquy, which in turn
birthed—a—soliloquy ... enlightening. However, here is the focus of
all this conjecture. My mask has fractured ever-so slightly, and in the
haste to recover its integrity I have found the truth of my journey.
My arc has brought me to the acquisition of the relics that hold my
fate ... Not one mask, but many; designed to succumb to the impact
of mortality, only to be replaced by another. Lament not for me. I
only understand the lamentation of others—I bare the world on my
back. The brittle bones heal with the astute acuity of Logan. My
genetic overlay, is a curse; only gifted to morosity's suckling.
Remove this curse I cannot—cannot ... I will not—will not, for it is
the order that has ledgered the strands of my destiny. Oh—you
jealous martyrs. So quick to cast your illusions into an ocean that is
merely a pond of your pontification. I beg you ... take this ballast.
Unleash this mast that I hold dear to me. I promise, you couldn't sail
a day's journey in that tub you label a body of water—without
cessation. This burden is not my burial, but my perpetual
resurrection in my auspicious indemnity. And here now, I ask not
refuge nor removal; only clarity. The fear, whether tangible or not,
grips me inconsistently. It suggests: "What lies beneath the final
mask, once this epic has reached its denouement?"

I Never Thought

I never thought I would be the monster,
That purges happiness
From those it was close to.

The pain in the pitch
Of the trembling voice ... is a mirror
That crumbles as it reflects you.

Embracing the feral jackal
That I am.
I adorn an enigmatic hide.

Reaching into the well,
That reservoir in my soul,
... confused by the good that lurks inside.

Just Scribblin

Face difficulty with satire.
Smile with a twist,
It dissipates like the Cheshire.

Understand I wouldn't know joy without pain.
It is dichotomy;
The epiphany is twain.

Letter to Daddy

I ain't really spoken to you in 5 years Daddy.
Walking through this world,
Homeward bound and all alone.
I ain't really know how to pen these ideas Daddy.
Trying to figure out,
How we even share chromosomes.

One of us is experiencing you for the first time;
Your natural clone.
I gotta look out for the one that's real emotional;
He ain't know you at home.
The other two are doing big things;
Their media's grown.
I'm answering questions, without the answers;
Still on my own.

Our gifts are transverse, frontal, and sagittal—
Che and I can turn the abstract into parables.
T's camera presence is captional.
E's athleticism and passion, at times, are untamable.

And J, well you know ... or you should have known—
He's the mastermind, whose work ethic is radical.

I can no longer be curt, Daddy.
I'm always stoic, but I'm starting to hurt, Daddy.
Feeling my brothers' pain, not mine,
Is the worst; Daddy.
We gotta talk before they put you in the dirt—Daddy.

Life is I-4

It's a wonder, I traverse this man-made territory.
The passage, writes itself off as obligatory.
A still mirage, above the asphalt,
Would have you believe this is the road to purgatory.
The anecdotes formed
On this motorway can be skewed,
So, I will purge this story.

Inevitably there will be a crash,
That halts the course plotted by the pilot.
But as Floridians, we've grown accustomed
To adapting to the climate.
The exits, at a glance,
Appear as images through an eyelet.
Persistence in the distance,
Keeps quiet that inner riot.

Viewing continuous pre-designed destruction,
Produces introspection;
Resulting in a moment,
Of shattered procrastination.
It's not often, that you get to look up—
From the route to your destination.
Realizing you're encapsulated
In a vault of imagination.

Forced to remain static,
In a vast sea of ingenuity and humanity.
Unknown if a journey on this path,
Reveals epiphany or calamity.

Salient Mirror

A prism—the ocean.
Refracting all of our thoughts.
Lost in the expanse.

Semantics

They ask if it's rap or poetry.
If I say yes, does it matter the flow you see?
Call it spoken word, bars, or epistemology.
Fundamentally rearranging philosophy.

Is it narratives or storytellin'?
Are we looking at cinema or television?
Anecdotes that extract decisions,
Forming protests; preformed collisions.

Communication of the highest accord.
Languages masterfully crafted—illusions implored.
Puppeteers or puppets pulling cords.
Ventriloquists or dummies echoing chords.

Looking for difference in deference.
Originality is borrowed creativity.
Recreations of regurgitated circumstance.
Our imagination is our reality.

Siamese Twin

From inception, we were complicated.
Not truly understanding the anomaly we were.
All outcomes were not contemplated;
Twain, without a symbol to differ.

Unaware that we are draining each other;
We would rather choose one of us to blame.
Truth is, we are that another.
All that we once were—trying to reclaim.

So now I cleave from whom I've been clung.
Not sure which one of us will survive.
No heroes in our war to label unsung.
No battlefield to salvage the shattered lives.

Sometimes the Devil is Me

Surely, it was Loki ... I tell myself.
This thought recurs, as I engage my task.
Shielded from ownership, I wear this mask.
Placed on the throne of denial itself.
Distanced all acts, as volumes on a shelf.
Enslaved to the carnal conquests, I bask.
My sanctum defiled, my self-choice is casked.
A resolution sided to oneself.
Yet, I was created dichotomous.
A being made of conscience and free will.
Truth—it is not always a deity.
No deed, no spirit ... that's anonymous.
The revelation, the foresight is shrill.
Now I see, sometimes the devil is me.

Steal Away

It is in this moment I am my most fragile ...
Witnessing mortality in its mature, yet infantile state.
We are born needing.
We die wanting ...
To hold on to the memories,
That at present—seem to be fading away.
You are a shell of the person I knew.
Truly a shell, soon to be clay—
Stripped of what it is that makes us human.
I hurt because I must.
These tears cleanse the image of you now,
And restore the past to the present ...
While defining the future.

Stoic

Sometimes, I lay back and look at the sky.
My dreams floating in a nimbus,
So many thoughts unbound and endless;
Visions replaying in a rhythmic high.

Peace and serenity, are the first that come to mind.
Remorse and anger push
Their way through the plume trying to engender—
Happiness, joy, and laughter soon I come to find ...
Loneliness, hurt, and a longing—
To all of these I surrender.

In these emotions, are a thousand decisions ...
Precipitated by a thousand incisions,
In the path I am trying to define.
The opening of doorways I envision.
The promises of others filled with rescissions;
One peak I descend as another I prepare to climb.

Staring at the horizon;
Piecing together the puzzle,
Outside of the box it lies in.

The Paradox of a Servant

This is my birthright.
Inasmuch, I understand its want and drain
On my soul.
Feast—
I allow you to.
Our cause ... You and I ...
It is our destiny.
You shall claim me one day.
And I offer myself willingly ...
I say willingly—
But it is not my will.
From this realization,
I am exhausted.

The Things We Value Most

From bartering to trade,
Of silks, rocks, and jade—
We've evolved to wood-pulp and diamonds,
No longer rumen.

Still in this day and age,
There's a market for slaves.
We still feed ...
Off of a commodity that's human.

Warrior Personified

When someone asks me,
"How far back do you trace your lineage?
"Aren't you from Africa?"

I reply ...
When I think of the mother land,
I remember holding my mother's hand.
She's the history; I've learned, rehearsed,
And come to understand.

Her name is Elizabeth Pennoh.
And she tells me about her mother.
The great, Yanforh Nyanwin.
So much so, that I did not name my daughter after me,
But after she.

You see—those matriarchs have made an arch,
To live on through my daughters.
I am not just a son,
But a conduit; a chosen one.
Whose mission wasn't only to be a father.

I am a knowledge bearer;
Molded to pass lessons to my children.
I had the greatest teacher.
Her examples informed my decisions.
Traversing the concrete jungle,
With a frame that is miniature.
Wisdom often revealed,
Through the finest of apertures.

I understood hard work,
By watching your daily grind.
Learned to persevere through the deepest of hurt,
Having witnessed your concrete mind.

Moments you showed the strength of men and mice—
Masterfully cooking Jollof rice.

Palm butter in the pot ...
And fufu too.

The smell of cassava leaves,
And plantains you cooked with ease ...
The fried chicken always hit the spot.
Ain't a mama as bad as you.

The nights of Vick's vapor rub.
The laughs we shared, that showed your love.
The correction and discipline—
That made your boy a man.

The days at church, I remember still.
The times you flashed your iron will.
You taught me to forgive myself of my sins.
I strive to make you as proud as I can.

You are a soldier of sustenance; in the kitchen.
An oracle; a prophetess—speaking blessings.
A healer, providing comfort I can rest in.
A mountain, whose peak I emulate in cresting.

Oh Nyusuah!

She is my rock by far,
Who has fought in many campaigns.
Wounded with many scars,
Across a field that's stained.

Until my dying day.
I will never forget the words you used to say.
... Staring into your battle tested eyes—
"Gnatee! Warriors don't cry."

Yahweh's Letter

As 1000 eyes look at me,
I am unsure whether they
Are accompanied by 500 smiles.
A disposition created by a duel between my narcissism
And the ideal society—
Traditions that have existed for a while.

Though they may think I have forgotten ...
I need you, to make it through.
Forgive me for the things I have done.
I have not turned my back on you.
Yet, I feel like a prodigal son.

It takes a tole to star in a role,
Directed by outsiders looking to play a part ...
Sifting through the negatives that are still developing,
I am anxious what the results will be.
I know David was a man after your own heart.
Is his fate the path I will see?

As I am burdened by forces external and internal,
I lean on the words my mother used to say:
"I never went to church looking for God.
God was already with me."—
Her voice is eternal.
I am aware I need your guidance.
I cannot let the chips fall where they may.

I have sinned, and will do so in the future.
I am in no position to judge others;
I cannot be a hypocrite.
I ask you to heal the impending wounds with a suture.
I am an imperfect person,
In constant search of self-discovery;
To this I do submit.

And in those times of living I don't understand,
I request an audience with you ... The Great I am.

About the Author

Brooklyn native Gnatee Doe, is a poet, author, motivational speaker, police officer, and U.S. Army sergeant who currently lives in Daytona Beach, Florida. Though he graduated with a bachelor's of science degree in Criminal Justice from the great Bethune-Cookman University, his passion has always resided in his minor in English.

In addition to studying the craft of writing, he also engages in outreach by speaking with at risk youth and organizing community events. Since the age of ten, he has found the pen to be the most effective way to express his perspective of life.

Other titles by Gnatee Doe: *It is My Time: The Anthology of Me*

Facebook: Convexed Cognitive Publications
Facebook: Gnatee Doe
Instagram: @convexedcognitivepublications
Instagram: @takeawalkwithme.3
Instagram: @themotivationmagnet
LinkedIn: Gnatee Doe
Twitter: @Gnatee Doe

Made in the USA
Middletown, DE
06 November 2021

51785119R00057